100 Landscapes

Coloring Book

Realistic & Picturesque Nature Outdoors, Beautiful Relaxing Beaches, Lighthouses and Rural Houses, Relaxation For Adults

Rachel Mintz

Join Rachel Mintz Printable Books Club
Members get notification on new books,
free coloring pages, discount coupons,
giveaways and more...   It is free to join - Scan below:

Colors Testing Page

This Book
Belongs to:

_____

_____

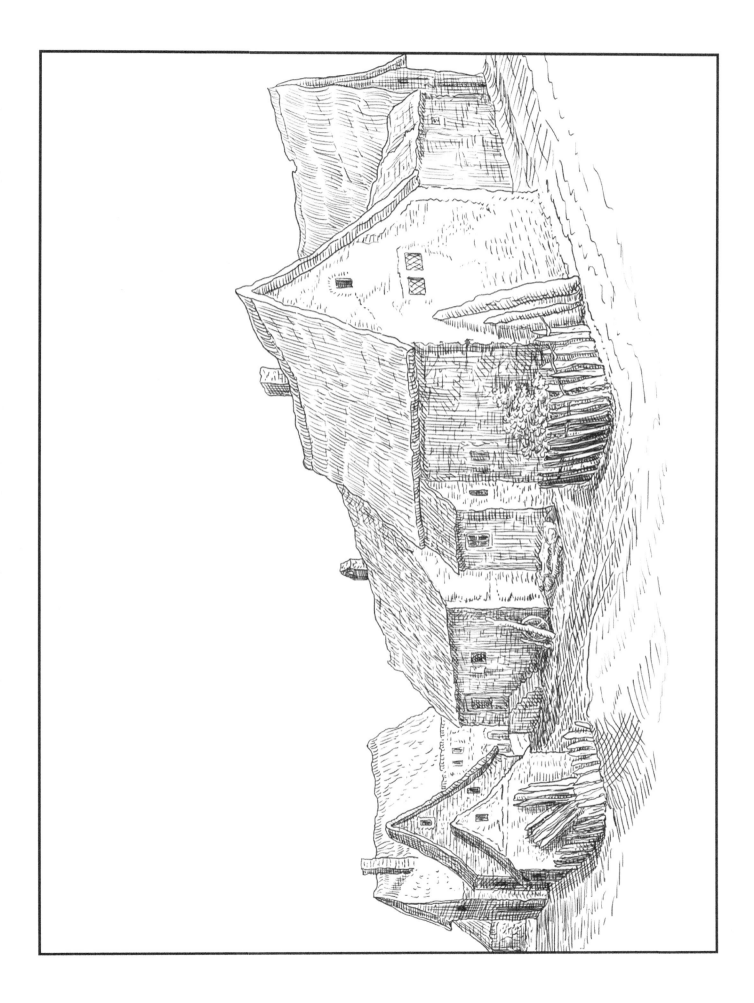

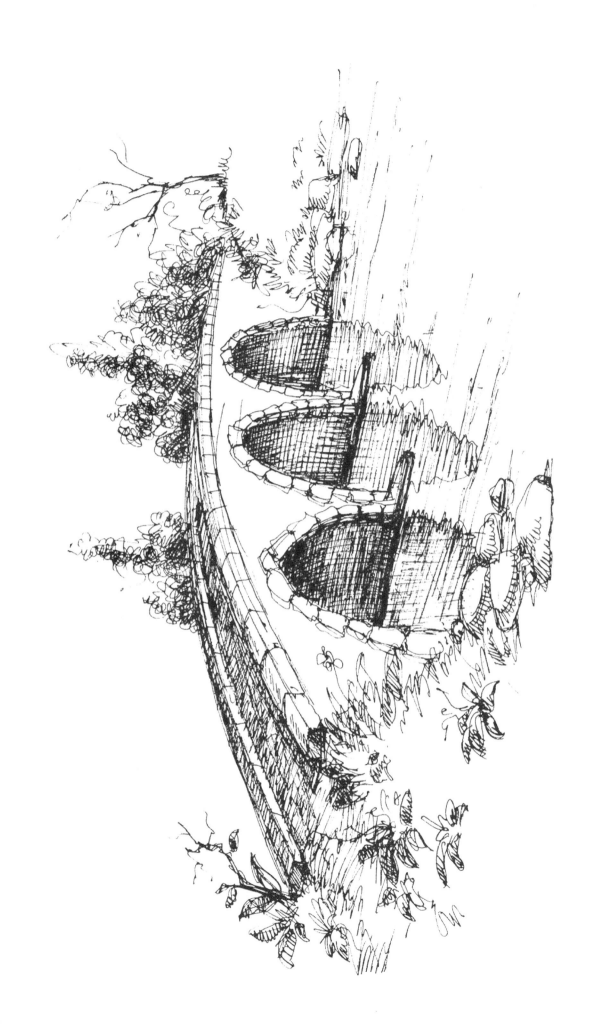

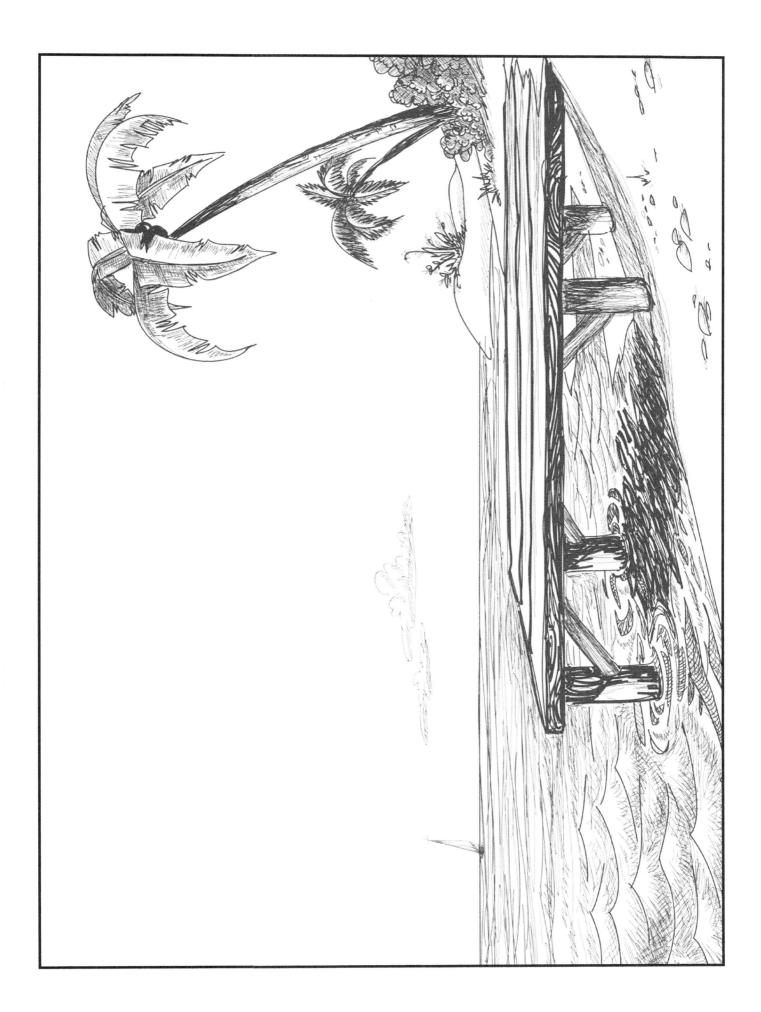

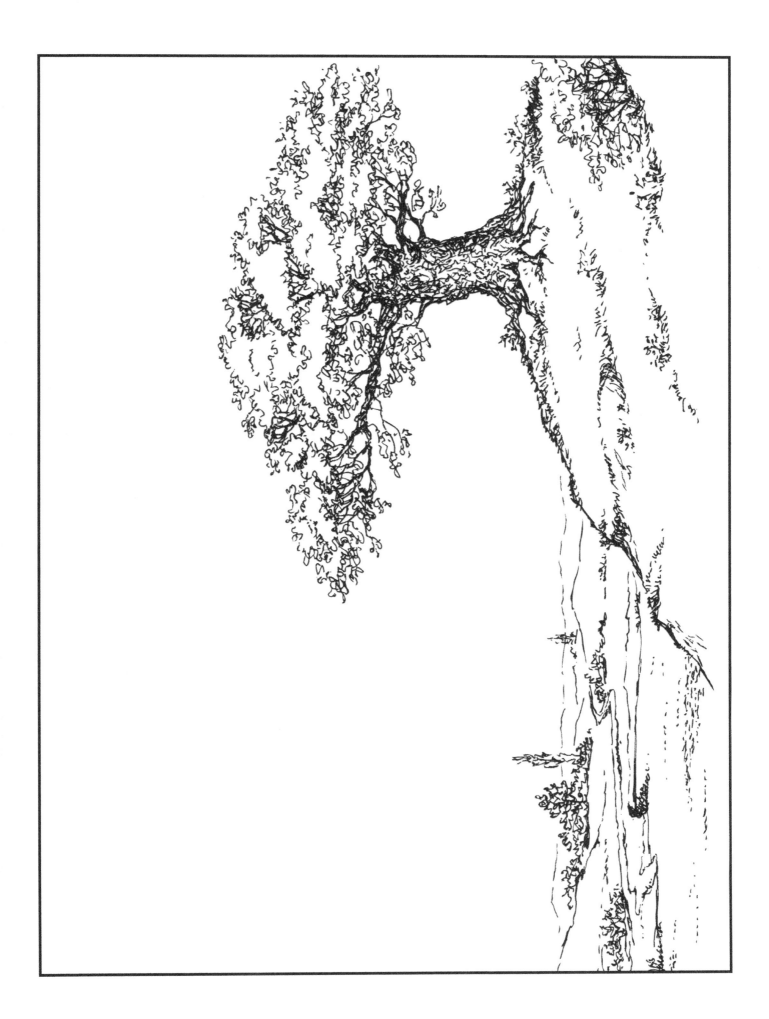

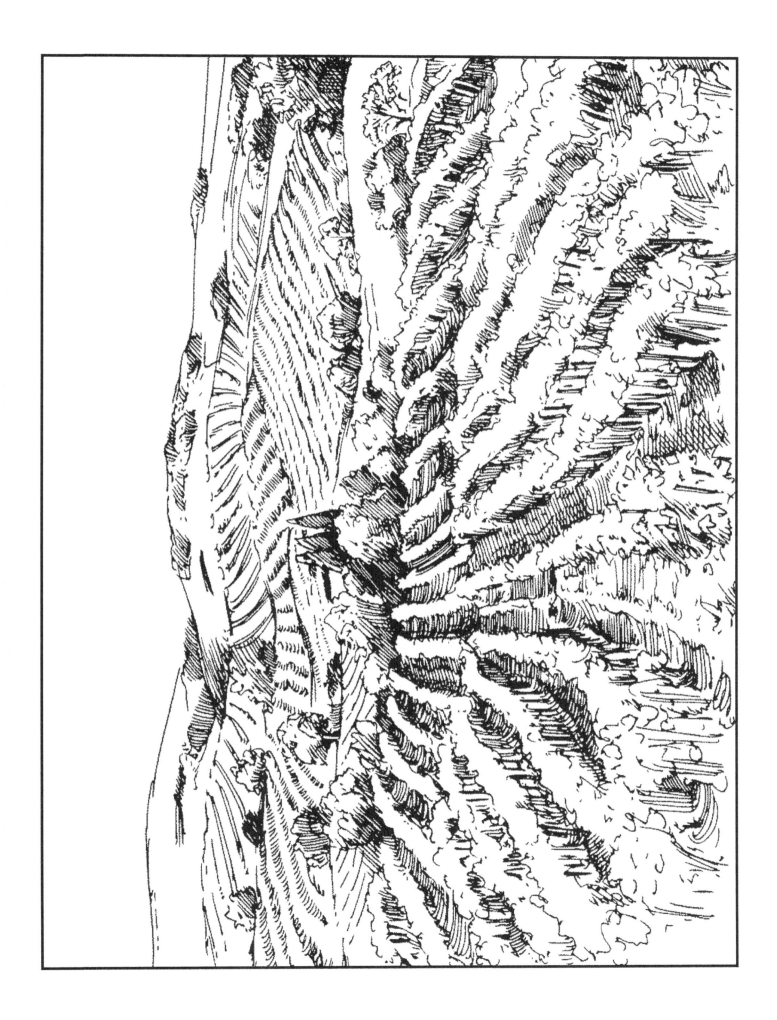

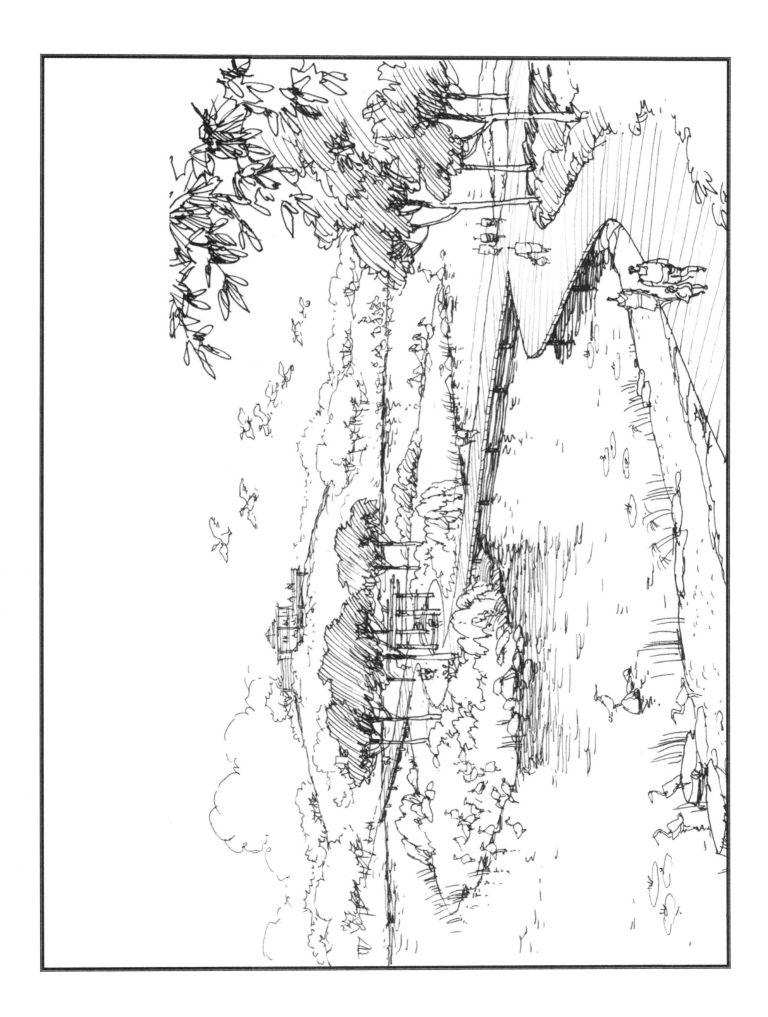

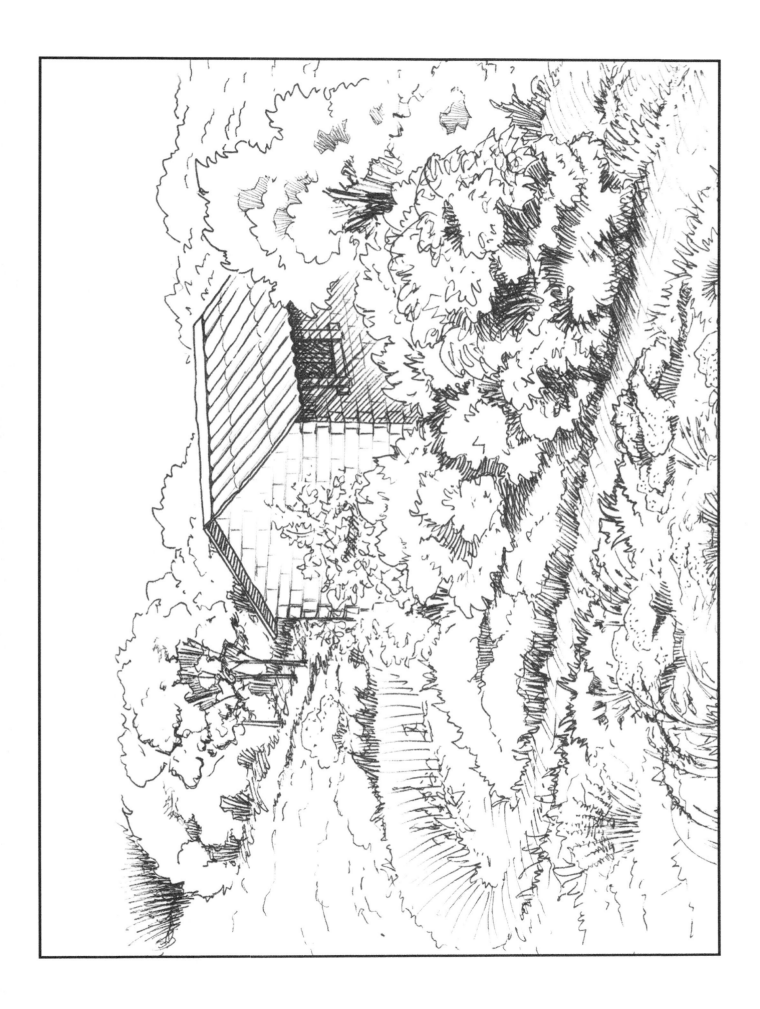

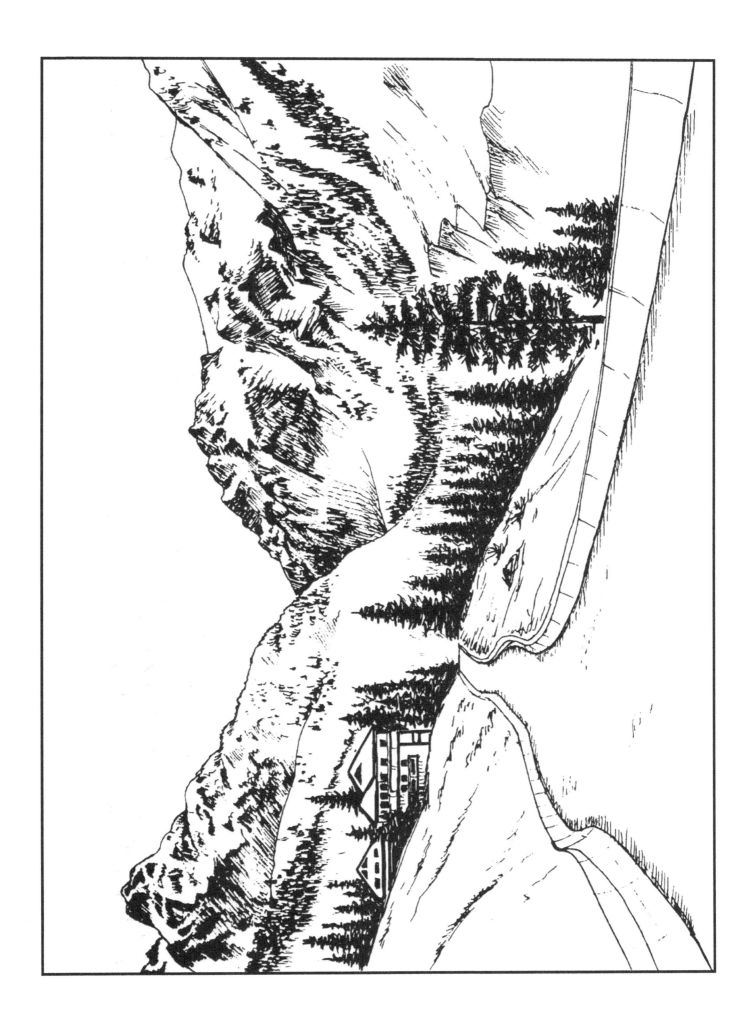

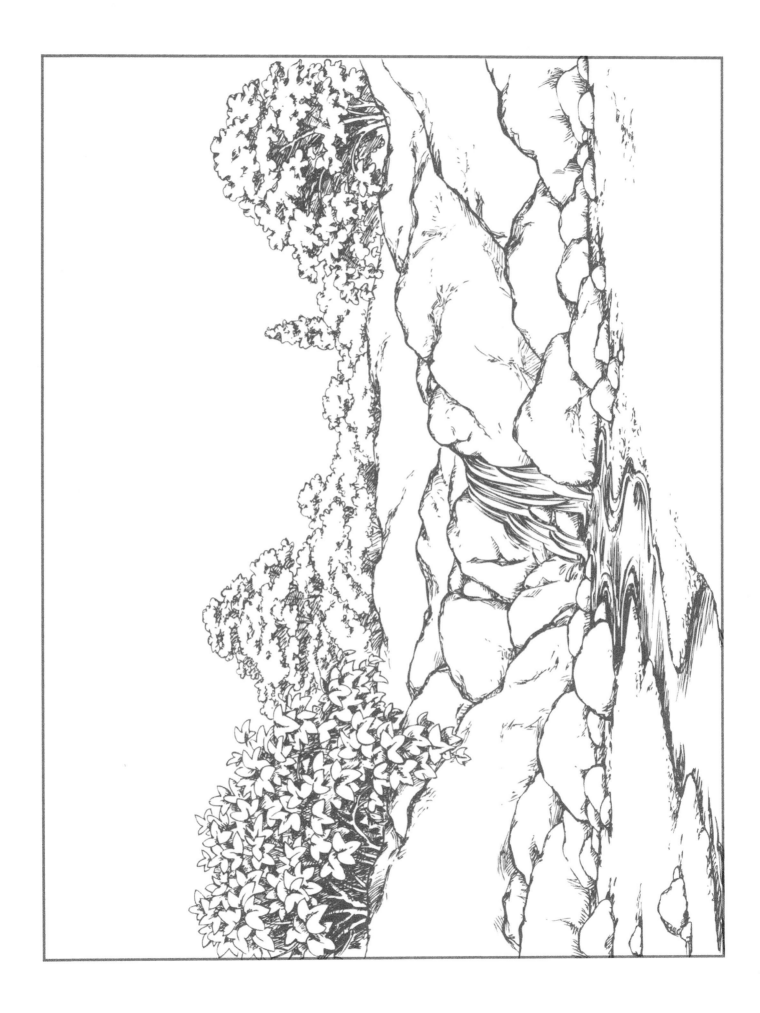

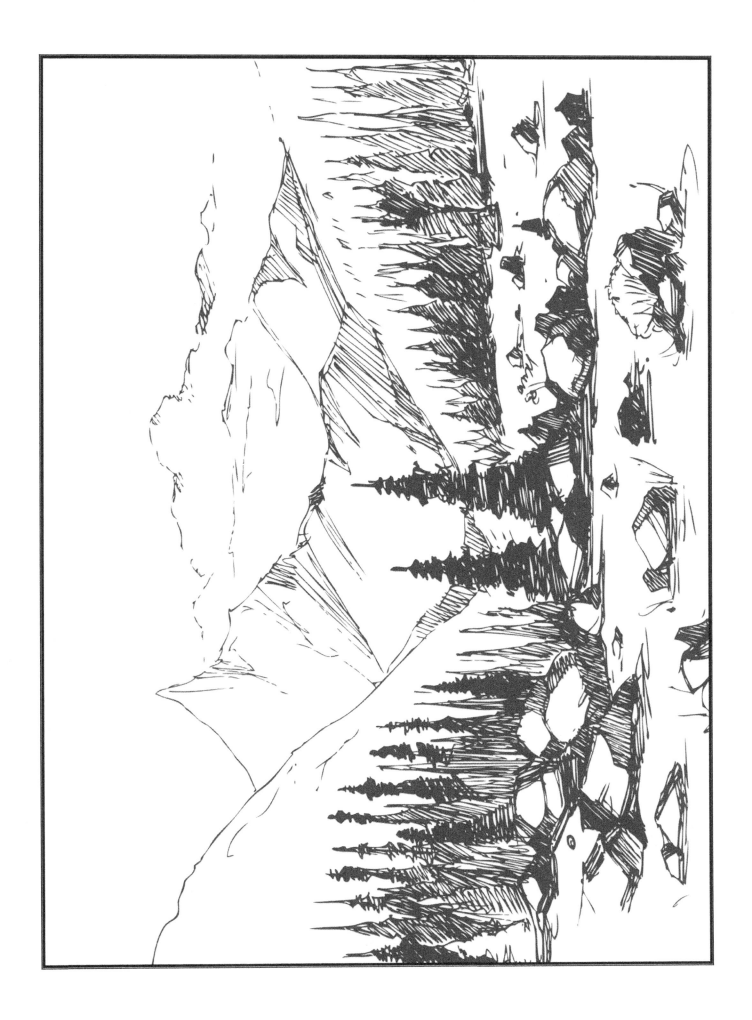

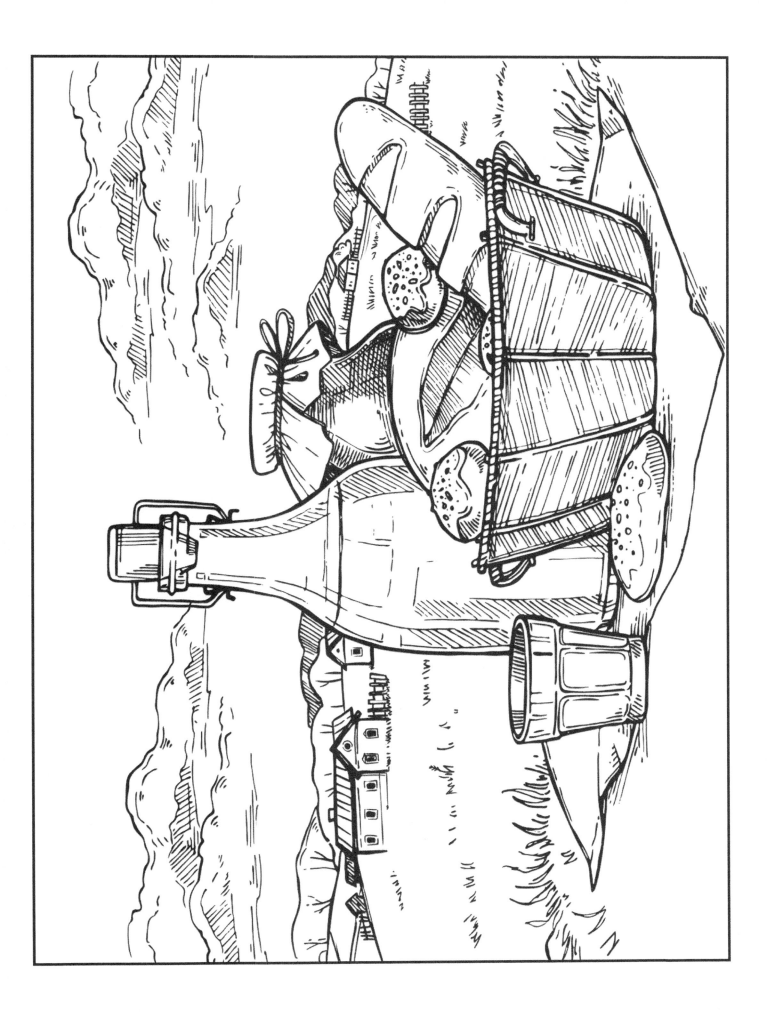

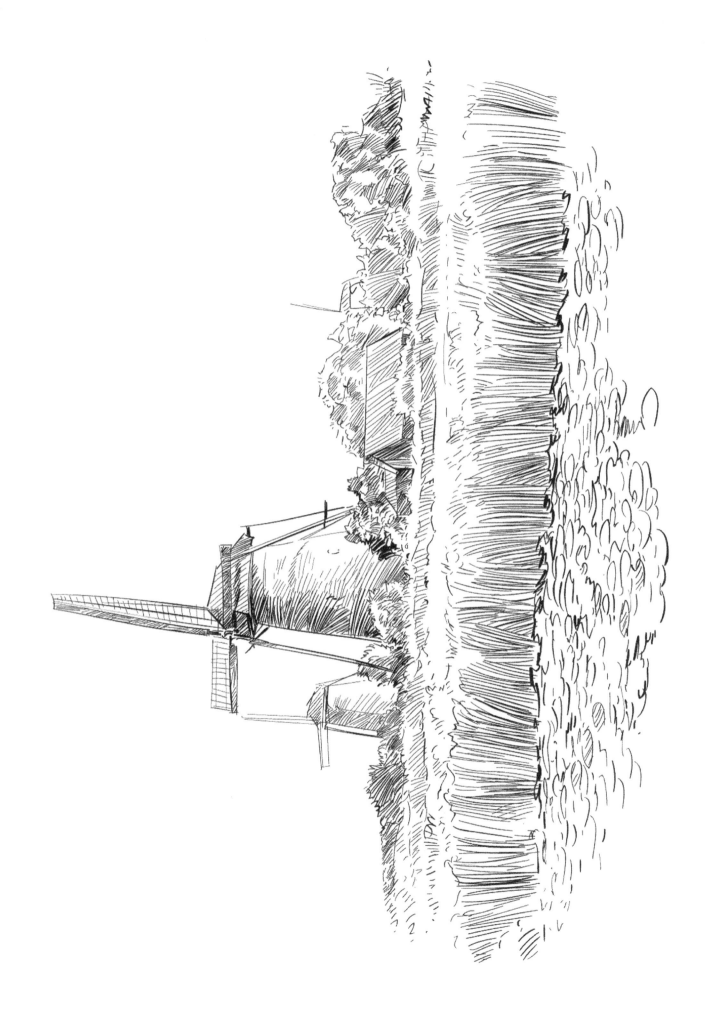

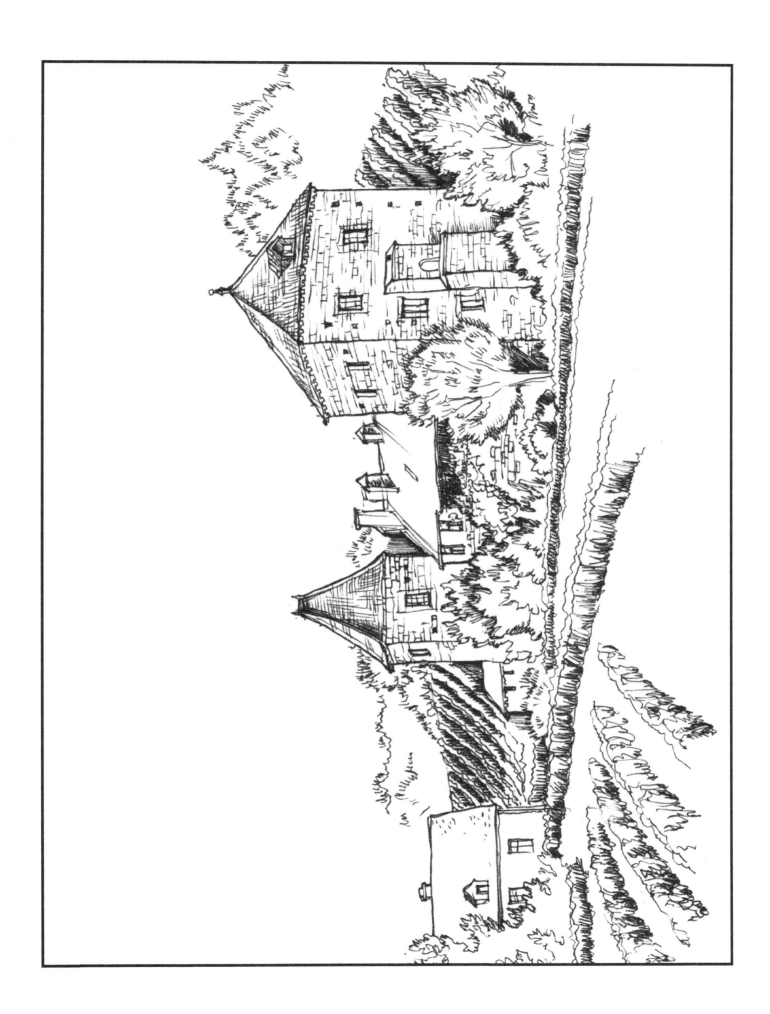

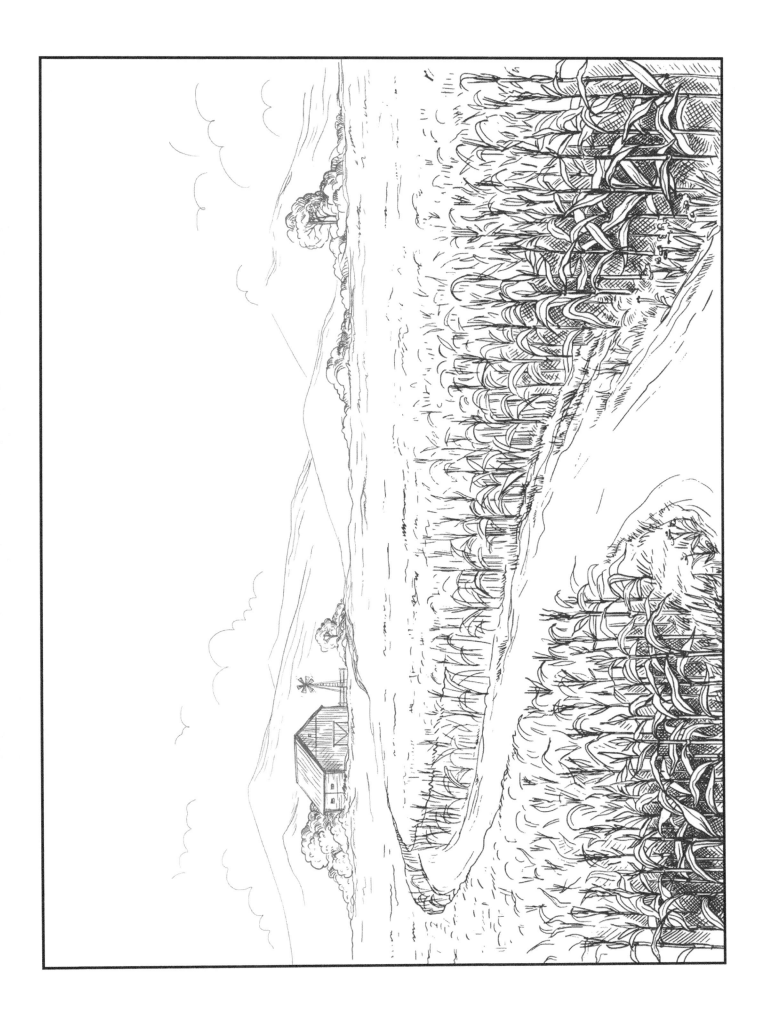

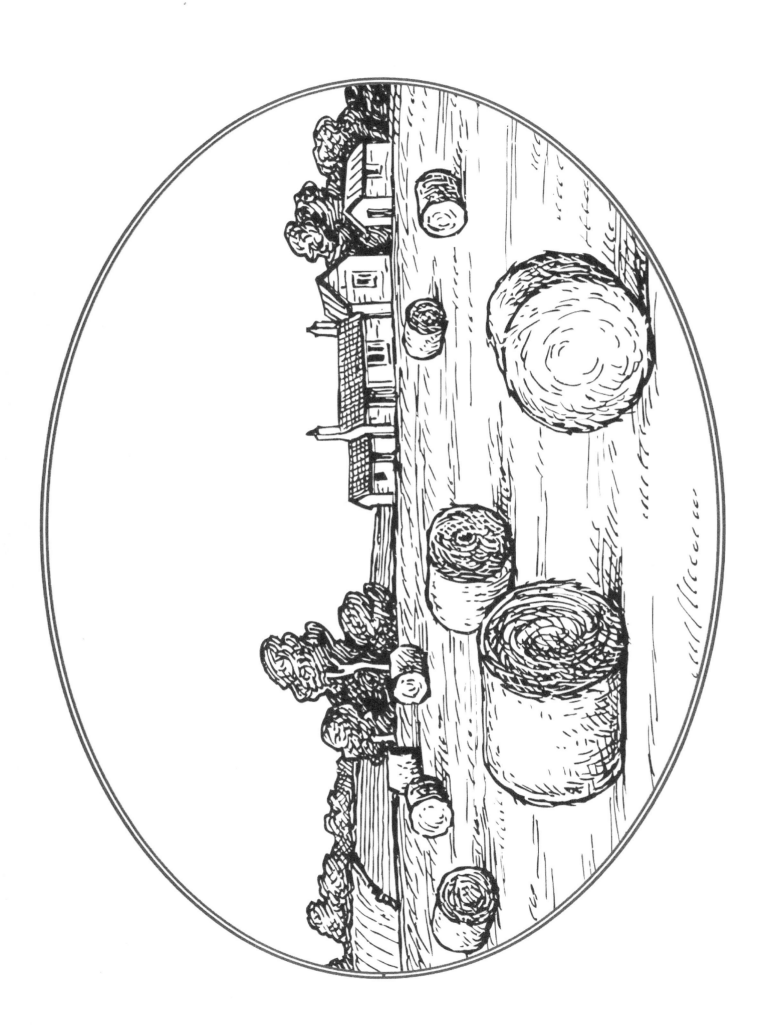

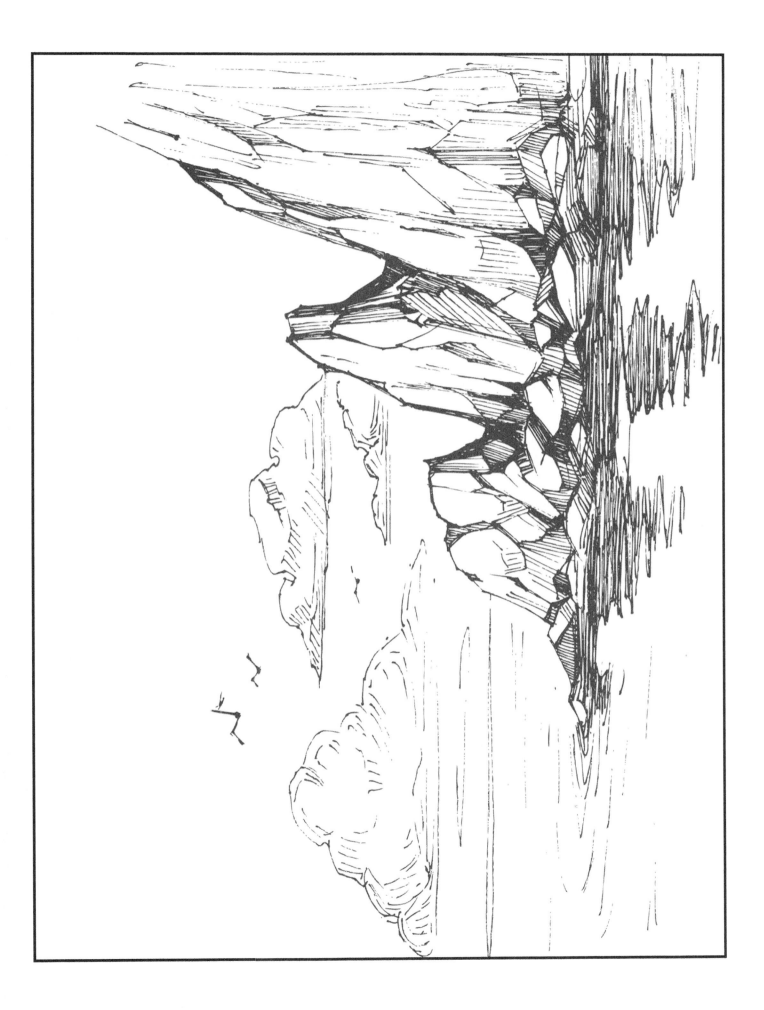

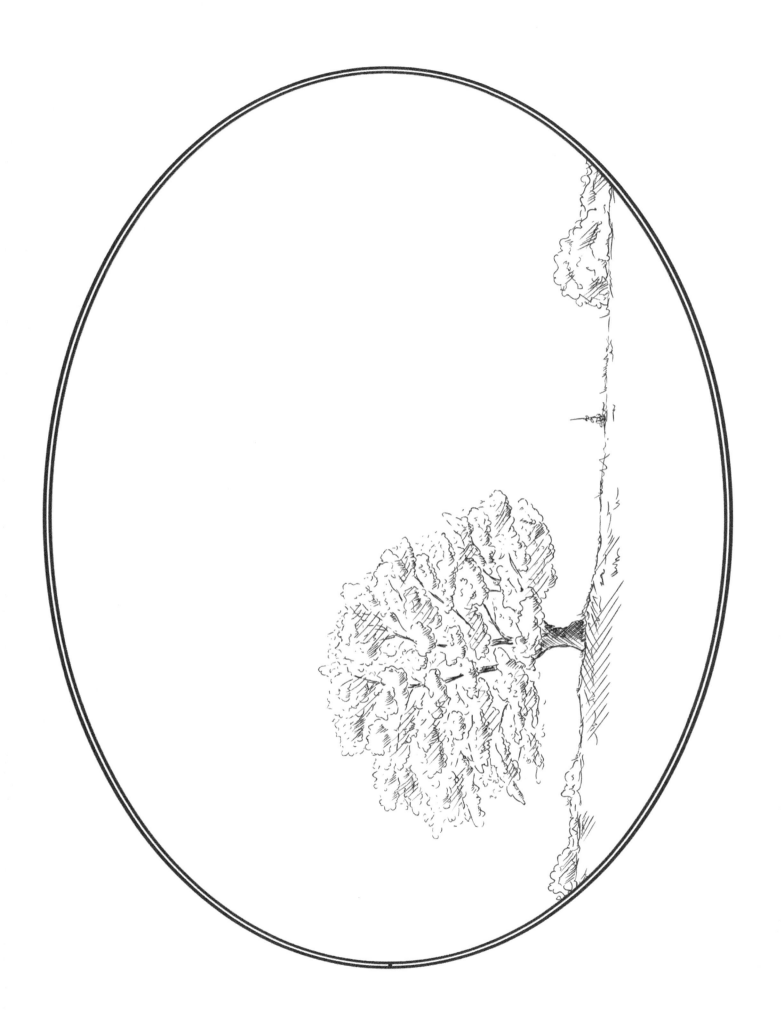

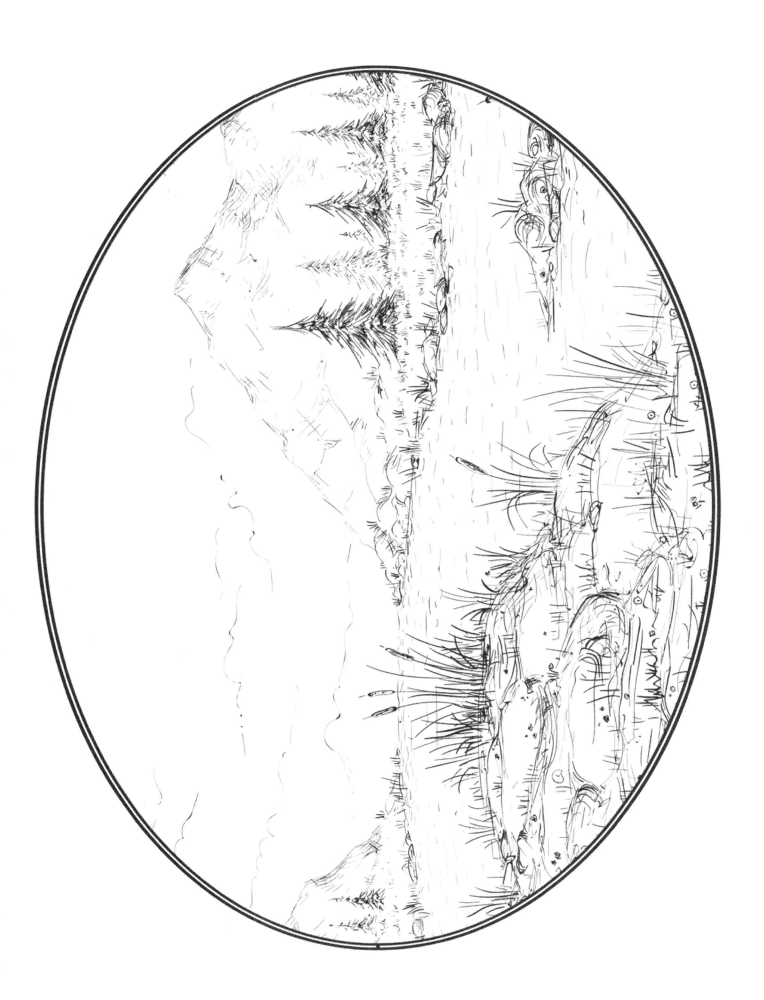

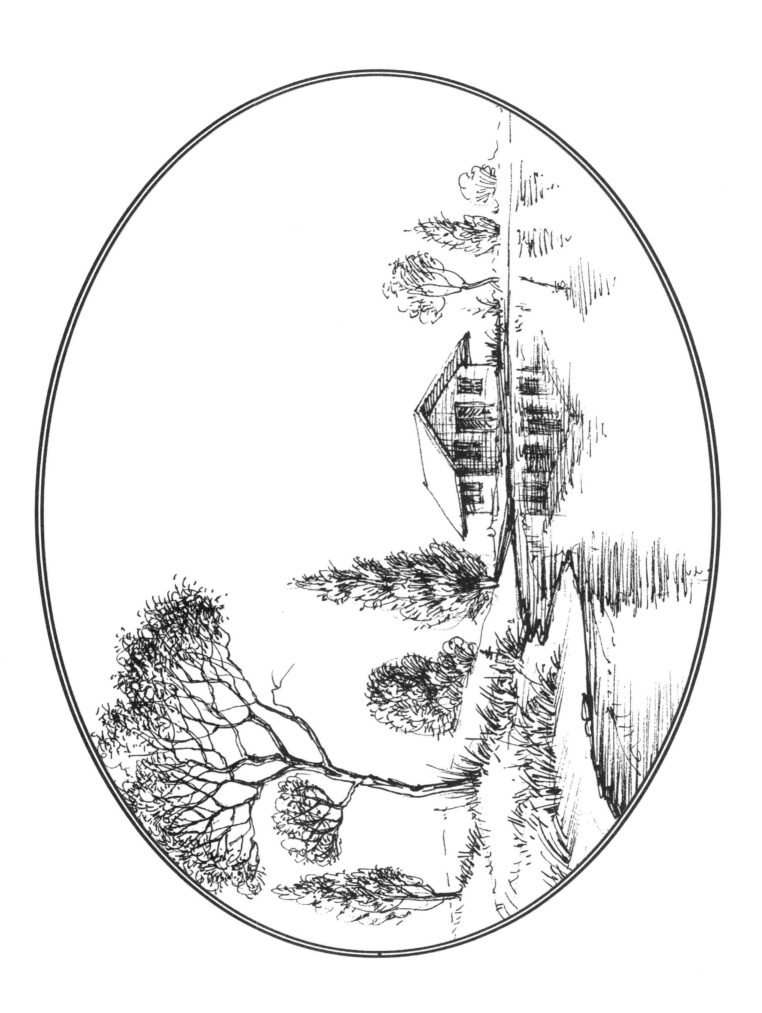

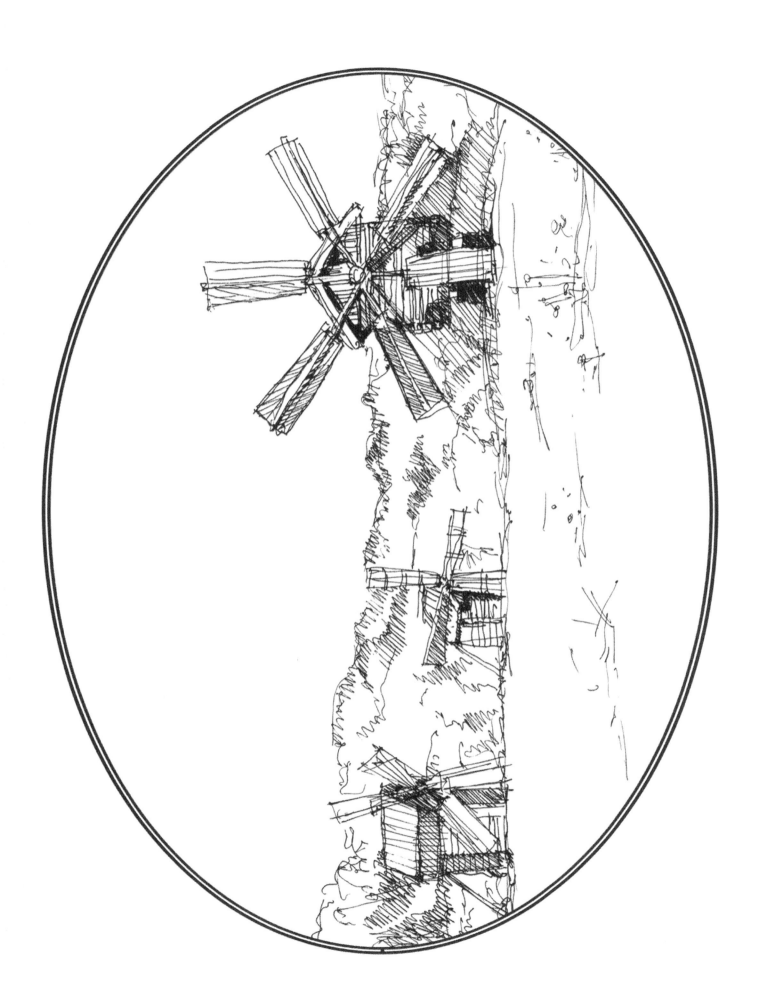

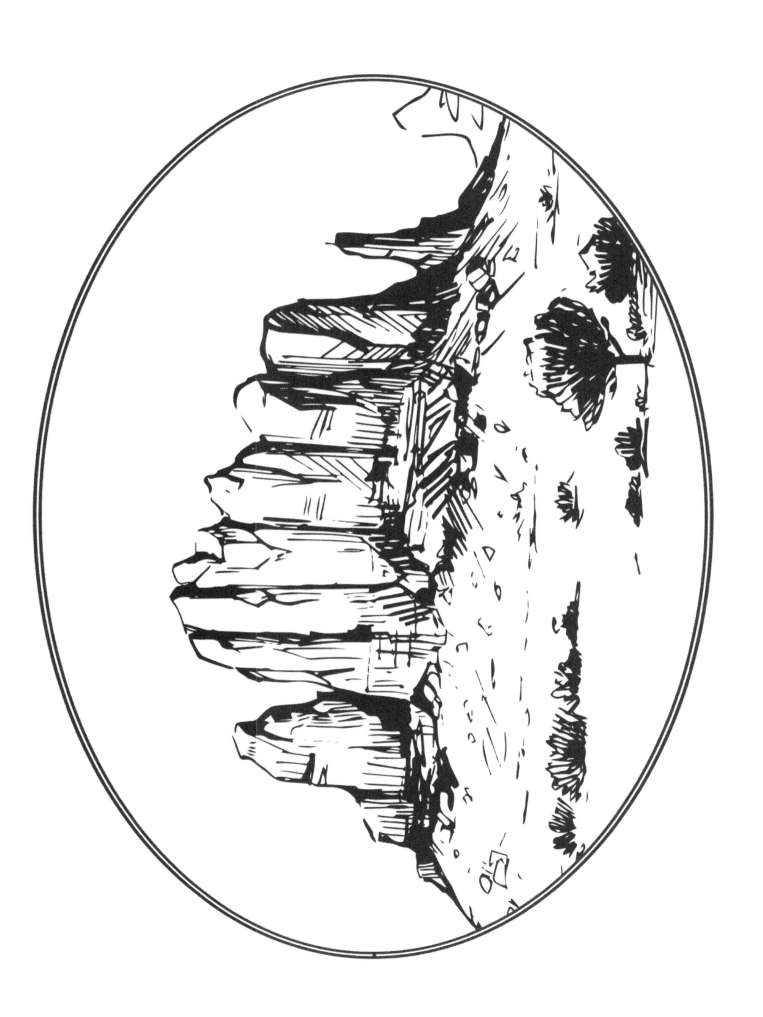

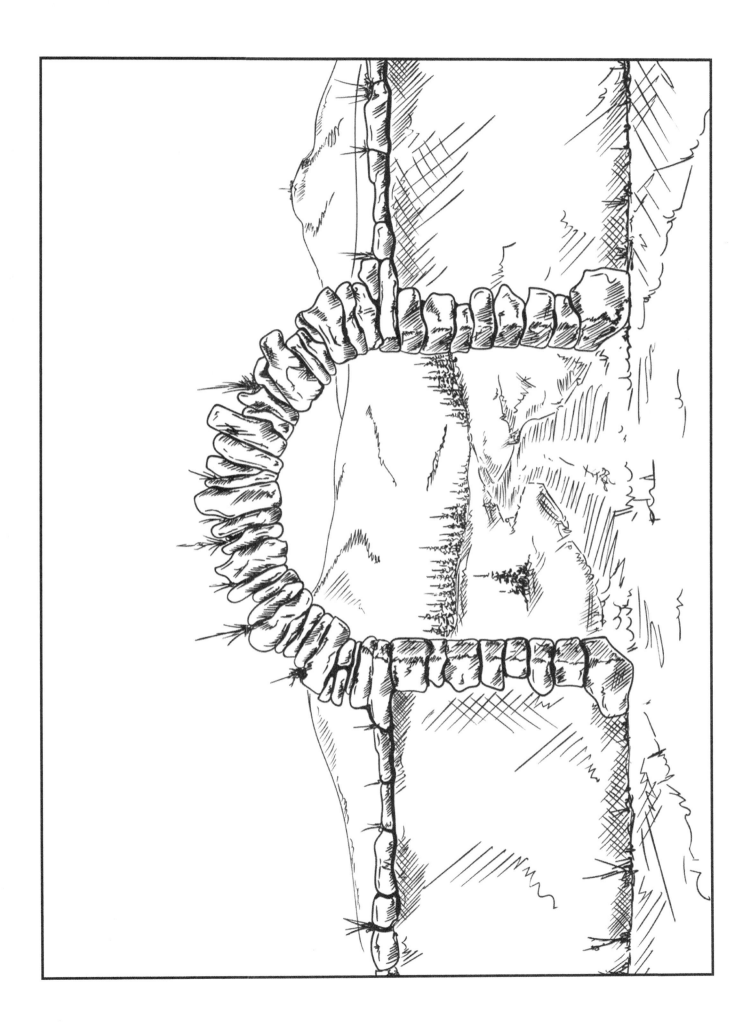

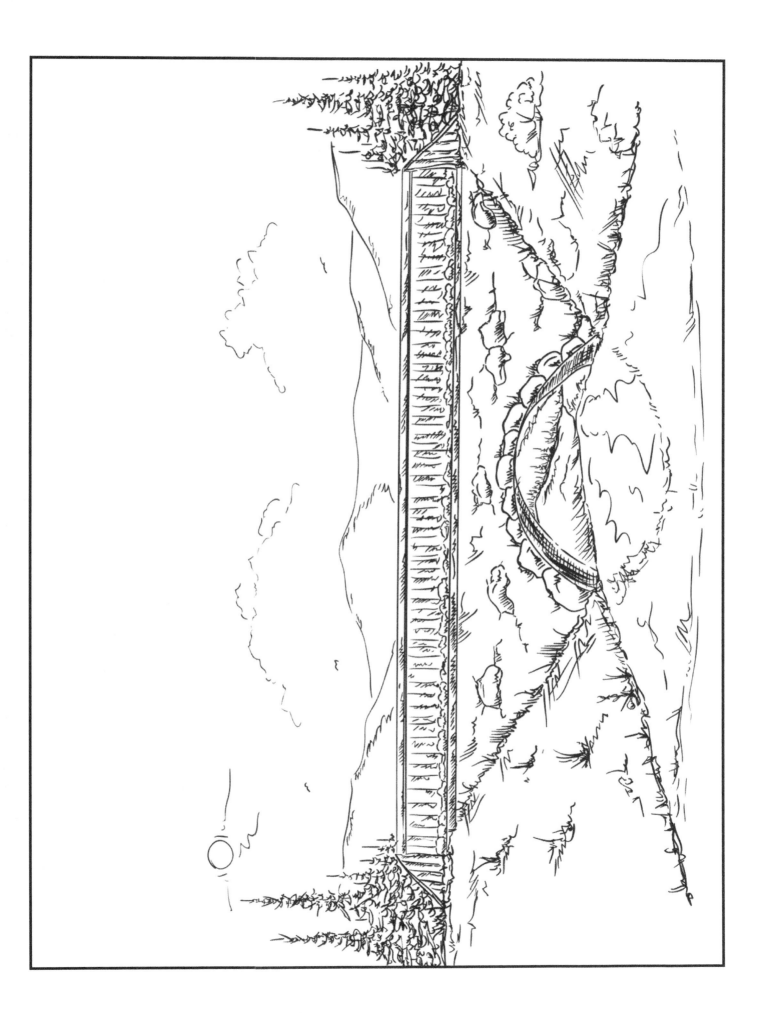

Thank you for coloring with us
We hope you had a wonderful time

For more Rachel Mintz coloring books to order on Amazon. Scan with your phone the QR codes on the next pages.

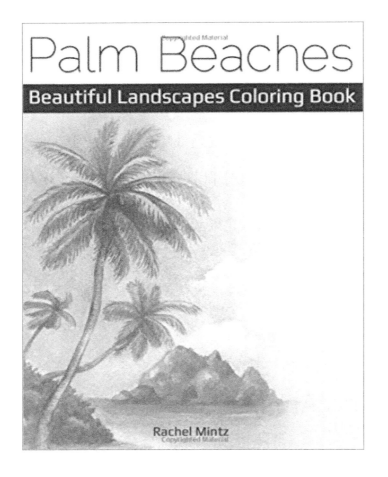

Scan to buy paperback on Amazon:

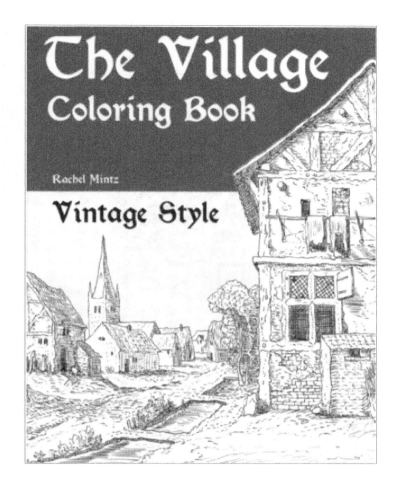

Scan to buy
paperback on
Amazon:

Scan to buy digital
printable PDF book:

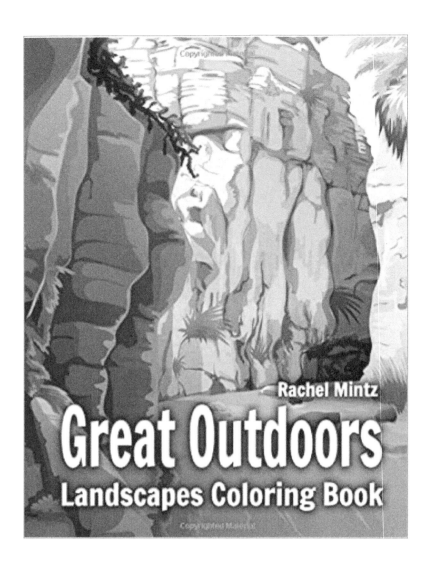

Scan to buy
paperback on
Amazon:

Scan to buy digital
printable PDF book:

Scan to buy
paperback on
Amazon:

Scan to buy digital
printable PDF book:

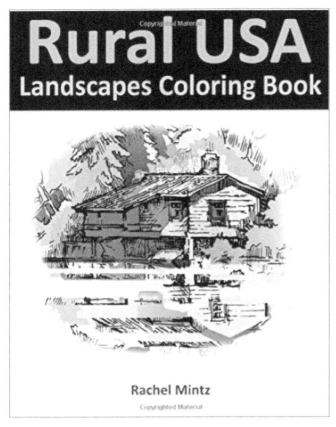

Scan to buy paperback on Amazon:

Scan to buy paperback on Amazon:

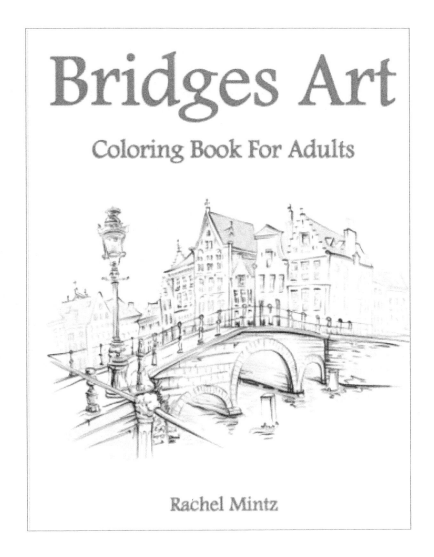

Scan to buy
paperback on
Amazon:

Scan to buy digital
printable PDF book:

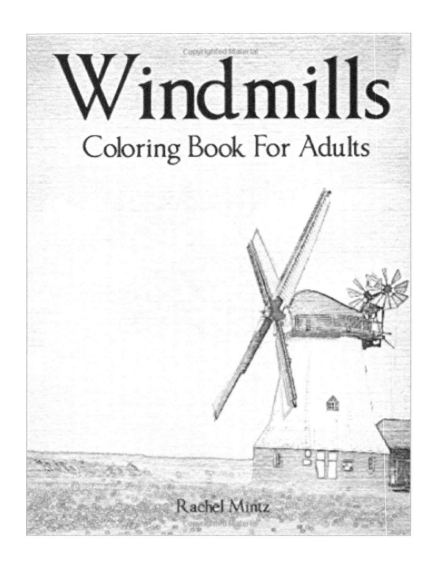

Scan to buy
paperback on
Amazon:

Scan to buy digital
printable PDF book:

Thank you for coloring with us.

We will be very thankful if you could
rate & **review** on Amazon for this book.

Add your colored pages to the review and show us
and everyone which pages you liked most.

Made in United States
North Haven, CT
16 May 2025

68938570R00122